Happiness is Hérault

About the Author

Edif Ava Rose is a seeker of the spirit of rejuvenation. She takes her writing quill and pens her soul's voice through words imbued with the sparkle of the light and joy of life.

Edif Ava spends her mornings in her writing snug in her country cottage where she enjoys creative writing, researching for future projects and reflecting on the magic of the metaphysical. This third book in the **Rejuvenate French Rose Poetry Series – Happiness is Hérault** has been inspired by summer sojourns to the Hérault region. A further two books in the series are available, **Perpignan Passion** and **St Tropez Senses.**

Having walked for two decades in corporate shoes it was time for Edif Ava to hang up the office courts and stride out in her own direction, to make her own unique contribution to the world. She hopes you enjoy this offering and if you would like to follow her writing journey look out for the other titles in this poetry series and the **Rejuvenation Buddy Series** that follows.

Happiness is Hérault

Rejuvenate French Rose Poetry Series

By Edif Ava Rose

ISBN 9781913560041

*This tiny treasure chest of happy
poems has been inspired by the
romantic, hazy, lazy days of beach
bears basking in the glow of the
Hérault sunshine.*

Happiness
is Hérault

Contents

Prologue to Happiness is Hérault

Loving all things Rejuvenate Rose Chic style I have taken my quest to various locations on the South Coast of France. These short sojourns have culminated in a suite of poems to celebrate the locations, the passions and people, opportunities for fun and fizz and to discover Rejuvenate Rose Chic on location. This is the third book in this poetry series, dancing in the Happiness brought forth on visits to the Hérault region and the surrounding area. Earlier books Perpignan Passion and St Tropez Senses in this poetry series chart a journey across the beautiful South Coast of France.

The department of Hérault contains within its borders and beyond a delightful mix of locations. From the beautiful Mediterranean beaches like Valras Plage, busy historic city centre of Montpellier in the neighbouring Gard region, Bezier, and the bustling port of Agde with accompanying naturist beach and resort of Cap d'Agde. Exploring further there is Narbonne and Carcassonne in the Aude region offering beautiful stop offs with Carcassonne's famous historic citadel welcoming tourists from all over the globe. A joyous amble along the Canal du Midi to the north makes for gentler sightseeing, the canal then sweeping out beyond the department of Aude towards Toulouse.

A visit to this area would start with a walk around Carcassonne where it is possible to be transported back to the time of the Middle Ages. If you're visiting during the annual fireworks, you'll see the citadel transform into a display of flames. Taking respite down towards the coast, you'll find yourself in Bezier the capital of the Languedoc vineyards. Here there are theatres, markets and out of town, lovely brasseries with shaded terraces to take shelter from the midday sun. But if sun and fun is your thing, then look no further than the heady sun-drenched sands of the beaches close to Cap d'Agde. Beyond the hubbub, time is well spent simply sunbathing naturist style and enjoying the feel of freedom when skin feels the caress of sun sea and sand. Further on inland can be found Pézenas a sweet place with a beautiful picturesque old town. Here you can find a market square, museum and abbey and cute little shops and artisan galleries. A particular gemstone atelier offered a joy filled keepsake of rose quartz to mark a beautiful summer journey of love and happiness.

Whilst there is much to keep the visitor entertained in Hérault, it is the light of a romance kindled in the town of Pézenas and the feeling of basking in the Mediterranean sunshine at Cap d'Agde that has birthed a free spirit, inspired to write these poems that proudly declare, 'Happiness is Hérault'.

Rejuvenate Rose
Chic

Les Poèmes – Happiness is Hérault

Boule de Cidre Sips

A welcome chance to explore Narbonne finds a beautiful
city with a pinch of glamour in the stylish shops
bejewelling the narrow alleys in the centre of the old town.
A daydream whilst sipping cidre and people watching
brings a sprinkling of spirit in the form of the Princess
Alialena born from a *'Perpignan Passion'*.

Sparkling those bubbles as they bob to the
surface,
chattering akin writer's mind as they stumble
and settle in space anew.

Shaded narrow streets cobbled earthy tones,
Daytime weary n' thirst for Princess mirage,
respite calling cooling liquid to quench.

A Narbonaise golden elixir hidden from
view,
hugged by earthenware bowl,
adjoining palms warming in reverent
embrace.

Aroma apple cute day dream inspired,
Green palm fronds wave in sun kissed stars,

alighting as gentle breeze welcomes their
gleaming motorised chariots.

Luxury lunch chic boutique style,
Narbonne carpet rouge spread fine and new.
Actress dressed in Majorcan shift Princess
come to life that Alialena manifest.

Autographs, thanks, gracious, replenished,
travelling forth on location,
Hérault vista sweeping, green and cypress
lined.
An aged villa prepared welcoming sparkling
stars to evening shoot.

Boules passed from one to another,
bubbling beverage enhancing co-star joy.
Evening breeze, cidre fresh tableau formed,
lines vine fruit ripe and ready to recall –
momentary mirage appears.

History of footsteps – romance born to book
to script to celluloid,
the light of life driven by her spirit settles on
director's shoulders,
writer's relief - idea birthed, inspiration
shared.

Romance à Pézenas

The inspiration for 'Happiness is Hérault' was heralded by
an evening stroll in Pézenas. The trip kindling the joy of a
romance enjoyed in the warmth and rejuvenating quality
of late summer in the South of France. After a late
afternoon repas, a stroll enjoyed hand in hand among the
art galleries, rock and gem store a special kind of bliss
cemented in a life's box of memories.

    Pézenas busy in the Hérault heat,
    treasures of early morning - flower baskets
    laid out,
    artist cave busy dressing precious creations,
    hopeful day's tourist discoveries turn to gold.

    Quiet calm descends après-midi,
    pregnant pause loaded with expectation.
    Town and folk readying selves,
    the heady warm charm of a mid-summer's
    eve beckons.

    Click clack of heels on cobbled stone,
    artisan's deep in distant chatter from late sun
    shaded ateliers,

echoes of romantic whispers,
lovers navigating old town.

Romance a tangible haze,
warm and thick hangs here.
Alchemy of late summer, a perfume of love,
its allure magnetic to followers from far off
lands.

Pézenas joy a prompt to remember,
wondrous moments of happy past,
love's memories mimic petals once adored in
full bloom,
a place time froze still.

A dream to return and hear whispered sweet
nothings,
clutching gift of rose quartz,
happiness and love from fond times,
those precious gifts of Hérault.

Bashful in Bezier

A trip to Bezier and surrounding villages with the same
name brings a sense of the true character of the Hérault
region. Bezier centre is set alongside a beautiful
boulevard of tall trees evoking the profile of the
Haussmann boulevards of Paris. Life is moving here in its
own rhythm and the visitor is drawn in to the intimacy of
this location feeling a gentle sense of being a foreigner
welcomed into a small city focused on its local lifestyle
and livelihoods.

    Boulevard wide and proud,
    an invite to Hérault vigneron capitale,
    impressing a bashful wanderer.

    Old and forsaken ghosts chill under generous
    shade of tree,
    talking through life's moments;
    a fate and destiny - what will be will be.

    Office hour folk quick step
    Traversing social and physical divide.
    French style luncheon makes its timely cry.

Wafts of mutterings float on air,
diners eat and savour vin short distance from
vigneron,
moments marked in time.

Bezier city in gentle flow,
visitors tentative in exploration.
No frenetic fever here but dynamics at play.

Locale arcane politique,
Subconscious vibe tickles surface,
les étrangers barometer engaged.

L'Amour de l'Été – Cap d'Agde Style

There is no place like Cap d'Agde. From the sense of
liberated spirit in the naturist village to the beauty of the
endless sandy beach, sun on the distant horizon and bluest
of skies. Enjoying summer romance in the Mediterranean
in this joyous place marks a poignant line in the sand of a
romantic life.

> Dreamy days as love sits in our embrace,
> air filled with romance, water and sand close
> by.
> Sunsets kissing long off horizons -
> butterflies we flutter with our pairing
> perfection.
>
> Swathed in sheer cotton, loin cloth and rose,
> attire in our smiles and winks of bosom and
> thigh.
> A nervous first meal generous salade,
> fruits refreshing and nuts banish hunger.
>
> Surprise hidden sous la table,
> bobbing buoys of bare chests,
> mouths move in song of restaurant
> conversation.

We steal ourselves in loving gaze for our
feast of adoration.

Hot sand engulfs skin and bone,
relaxation and smooching mood we wear like
body halo.
Ridiculous goings on ignored a glance away,
nothing to disturb bear cub snuggles.

A lasting memory of swinging hammock,
sleep in heat and haze,
our movement in time two into one,
a single heartbeat of summer romance.

A Carcassonne Feast

One of the most popular stop offs for tourists in this part of the South of France is the compact medieval citadel of Carcassonne located in the Aude region that sits alongside Hérault. Famed now for its fireworks and illuminations display alongside Châteaux Comtal, the fortress and its maze of ramparts and bailey and Basilique church of St-Nazaire. Musée-Lapidaire de L'Abbaye de Gellone with its archaeological remains and the Musée des Beaux-Arts that counts works from French, Flemish and Dutch masters, including Corot amongst its collection tempt a pit stop tourist to return. This place takes you through the arrival of crusaders, rebellions and subsequent decline when Perpignan took its place in guarding the region. Thankfully grand restoration works were carried out in the nineteenth century when the Romantic movement brought medieval sites back to popularity. Romance still alive as a location to Rejuvenate Rose Chic style…

Heavenly heat caresses stones beneath,
winding upwards medieval path to citadel.
Parched we stop - easing thirst and feet,
ground toes and muse in mellow touristique
méditation.

Eve stretching forth five stars beckon,
dressed in finery discussion elevated with topics
opportune and apropos.
Joyous anticipation of clinking glass,
deepening wave of union romantic gaze our anchor.

Four courses fabulous, frivolous champagne and
roux dresses pescatarian feast.
No cassoulet winter nourishment this day.
Lost temporarily in high day holiday fayre,
fromage, chocolat, espresso - ritual and gourmet
delight.

Carcasonne feast a memory treasured,
appreciation flowing euro style.
Jewel of small city wrapped in its walls,
silhouettes lit up against star blue of late summer
eve.

To slumber we go, the cities essence wafting
through the rhythm of tall French shutters.
Mimicking in candle light flickers.
The romance of images this night,
theatrical backdrop to our nocturnal sleeping stories.

Dreams casting everlasting spell -
an imprint on the soul.

Dancing with night fairies, skipping o'er cobbles and
alighting stairwell.
Come to balance together atop city wall,
to linger a while and admire human summer souls
sleeping deep.

Sun, Sea and Sand at Valras

When on holiday away from normal routines the call of
the beach is always on one's mind. The long fine sandy
beach of Valras-Plage will tempt you just fine. A short
drive south from Bezier, there exists a quiet seaside spot.
A little fishing port and yachting harbour at the mouth of
the Orb carries the long beach to the Grau de Vendres and
on to the Aude region beyond to the west. You can seek
out the Théâtre de la Mer (Théâtre Molière) in Sète or take
to the sand and water where the sun throws down its warm
blanket of heat and light, enlivening skin and serenading
you Rejuvenate Rose Chic Style ….

> Happiness threefold veritable delectation,
> Valras delivers.
> Basking, bronzing, beautiful,
> all cares forgotten.
> Special moments stretch across time.
>
> Warmth radiates from every surface,
> sun's rays the source of all joy.
> Resplendent light emitted, nourishing all
> souls.
> Energy of pure spirit bathing all hearts.

All we have, all we are, happy hearts – that's
all we need.
Relief in realisation o' that universal truth.
Self-sufficient right place and time,
perfection to just be.

A paddle, a dip, submerged salty waves, life
force awakened, movement and flow.
Sea water envelopes, lapping at floating self.
A special kind of contentment,
lone water-babe in mermaid mellow mood.

Sun and sea – sand completes triple delight.
Golden grains mimic time,
sifting away fear and pain,
troubles all distant memories.
And now - Valras happy, under sun, beneath
sea and atop hot heavenly sand.

An Italian Abroad

Europe seems to be a melting pot of knowledge and understandings, sensibilities and lens-coloured hues through which life can be lived. Those individual countries and principalities unite to make a wonderful caldron of multilingual inspiration for industrious, scientific and academic pursuits. For those creative souls, if they choose to wander the continent and follow the signposts in life they will be led to great wonders and works - then perhaps strangely back to their own truths.

Hérault seems an unlikely spot for sophisticated Italian holidaymakers but the siren call to naturist soul brings them to rest a while on the sandy beaches. Their style and elegance enhancing ambiance, conviviality and enjoyment for all who draw near. Inspiration from this Hérault snapshot in time beckons me to craft a dreamy tapestry of stories of an Italian Journey to Find Love. For now, some footsteps in the sand ...

Passagiata Italian Style,
onward to horizon Méditerranée,
evening sun and infinite happiness.
Is there nothing more joyous or generous?
Arms entwined with an Italian abroad.

A fish in its water when summer heats,
finest body suit for seasonal far niente.
Broad shoulders held proud,
no resting place for ego here.
A life well lived on cusp of twilight.

Bears bask on sun-drenched beach,
two bodies one, reality galaxy away.
Time parked at airport terminal,
that luggage of life left behind.
Sand pours betwixt fingers, toes and paws,
warm memory burnt into souls.

Prizing bears from sandy spot,
sette hora gentle libretto riposte 'too soon!'
Moules frites and champagne effective bate
beckons discerning appetites.
Single moment passes, attired,
refined, bejewelled and gleaming.

Restaurant a sea of European splendour,
wealth shadowed and opulence mere hint.
Glowing evening boho fashion suffice.
Sunset a backdrop to that eating theatre.
Steps forth her Signore – her dream una possibilità?
Italian abroad, a bear on the beach no more.

Returning to natural habitat a heartfelt pain,
till promise of return.
Leaving something of their soul those beach bears,
feeling as one beyond time and fearful finality.
Memory held till twilight's end –
reality aware, conjunction evolving two separate
intents.

Couscous in Cap d'Agde

Cap d'Agde is a wonderful promontory that has been developed in recent times to provide a busy and bubbling seaside resort. It is one of the best sites along the Languedoc coast with several marinas public and private boasting over 1000 berths. Space fit for the glitterati and amateur yachties alike. Architecture fashioned from the traditional Languedoc buildings with some holiday apartments decorated with pastel walls and tiled roofs reflecting beautifully in the waters of the harbour. Other winding streets lead to the piazzas for holiday merriment and native celebrations. Seeking out a little historic culture at Musée de l'Éphèbe one finds a magnificent bronze statue of a Greek man, nude but for vine wreath around his head and remnants of a tunic or soldiers shoulder padding. It's titled Éphèbe d'Agde. It's not much of a stretch for the imagination to see how this statue may inspire those seekers of spirit and adventure to make a detour from common tourist path to one of the largest nudist colonies in Europe to join les naturistes. Holidays here awaken, enliven and tease a curious spirit for the light where days stretch out, views amaze and hearts sing songs of the joy to just be, aux natural style! From even this, a respite back to normality is needed in the form of Couscous sustenance….

Sun drenched days where energy drains,
Fluffy sustaining vin d'Agde fayre beckons.
Lime and fruity couscous with fish heaven sent
succour,
Sweet sultana and zest sharp, palate refreshed.
Cap tourist chatter bubbling in that summer like no
other.

Restaurant cute amidst busy bar lined port,
vibrant colour cool tiles to soothe,
environ fun filled with summer day antics.
Dog tethered, sun drenched heels it laps,
sleepy heads from heat disabling verve.
Calmness amidst carb-fuelled chatter,
his deep sigh of joy in that summer like no other.

A few moments shared,
respite from crowds impeding segways,
mood matching canine a gentle fatigue enjoyed.
Evening silk dress billows on this unusual eve,
some focus, words and meaning laid bare.
Summer romance drifting towards horizon of time,
a summer like no other.

Love and adoration - dog and man alike,
fearful, frenetic crowd distraction, normal life
dancing on the fringe.
Couscous consciousness prompting return, hand
over hand a public declaration.
All is love, that summer like no other.

Surreal days dreamy and unreal,
regional sport watching fun and frolics,
ruffling o' people's feathers.
Éphèbe d'Agde inspired – majestic n' tall,
at one and dressed in skin and oil,
only sun's barrier morality factor.
Cap d'Agde a place to see and be seen -
world renowned unusual corner of earthly pleasure.

A sheer joy and sweet table talk,
giggles shared, people watching fun and day's
moments recalled.
Canine ears peak at mini treat.
That summer like no other,
morsel treat a detour from steadfast endurance
driven lifelong.

Espresso to energise segway return,
heat of the evening a gown worn with relish.

A match for conscious couscous cooked light and
fluffy,
that squeeze of lime a promise for night time
pleasure to come.
Sharp and precise kisses – very special that summer
like no other.

Moules Montpellier Style

Montpellier in the neighbouring region of Gard is a charming capital to Languedoc-Roussillon boasting attractive historical districts, wonderful gardens all set alongside the modernity expected of all vibrant French cities. There is a dynamism here which is driven by its role as the administrative centre for the region and the history of university life alive and buzzing today. This city dances with a youthful vibe that speaks of its late arrival on the historic map. From its sale in 1349 to the King of France by the earlier John III of Majorca and the inception of the medicine schools that evolved into the university in the early 13th century. In modern times this place has evolved to encompass new residential suburbs and focusses its development in laboratory medicine, big pharma, local farm production, media, tourism and leisure. A truly multi-faceted place.

The verve and wealth of this city is now epitomised in the contemporary structures like the conference, concert and shopping centres. A spot of city people watching and exploration of a new place rejuvenates and revives, Rejuvenate Rose Chic style. This short trip to soak in the vibe a welcome break to a sun-drenched summer stay…

Mellifluous moules in garlic butter,
crisp frites accompaniment,
sparkling those bubbles in wine so fine.
Montpellier afternoon sun soaked,
pavements scorching soles.

Sun's hue and pigment,
a match for life's canvas.
Deux moules in Montpellier,
odd shellfish inside n' out and about this
capital Languedoc-Roussillon.

A grown-up kind of organised,
this city sharp, dynamic, neat.
Scholarly legacies to architectural delights,
an Occitan order and business set out,
clear and absolute.
A café serré to end that moules summer.

Feast enjoyed a walk to enliven,
two hands held, hearts dancing.
Souls not quite entwined that day but
curious,
a kiss to sign understanding betwixt.
Gratitude for life's pleasure a moment
worthy to mark.

Youthful tourists soak in style,
marvelling Montpellier wonders.
Wandering affluence their backs straight,
elegant refined rich uniform on display.
Maillot de bain signature stripe peaks
beneath,
akin those memories o' summer wine red
and white.

But this too - detour to arc of lives,
deux moules side by side for moments true.
Resting in plot reflect and wonder,
what mellifluous moments marking a
summers end.
Montpellier style, a joy to fulfil.

Hazy Lazy Days in Hérault

Hérault at its source comes from the river Hérault rising
on Mount Aigoual and falls downhill to the Valleraugue
and beyond. From chestnut trees to whole orchards on to
vineyards and olive groves the vista is replenishing.
Beyond Pont-d'Hérault to Pont du Diable the river lands
on the Languedoc plain. This region similar in size to the
Pyrénées-Orientales further down the coast past Aude,
spans from La Grande Motte and Montpellier to just
beyond Valras Plage. The pretty town of Pézenas, the
festival city of Bezier and Agde old town to the beach
resorts of Sète and Cap d'Agde are highlights on a holiday
sojourn.

Here holidaying is a serious business attracting tourists
from far and wide, sunshine, fun and pleasurable pastimes
on offer, one can find a memorable stay to while away
hazy, lazy days on a quest to satiate a thirst for
Happiness…

Sunsets wide and glowing,
that Mediterranean light kissing our
countenance,
hearts full, minds and bodies as one,
yielding thoughts befitting hazy time.

Energia solare enriches bilingual pair,
lingua amore union amidst those lazy days.

Adam and his Eve alive in Hérault,
nature the beach uniform to while away
moments.
Time stretching, bending, curves and
contracts.
Nothing measurable but heave and sigh of
release – heart's tensions set free, una
liberazione.

Time and fear seem forgotten,
this far-flung corner Français with its
carefree agreement to just be.
A landing place for naked bears
stripping away conformity,
everyday life in the distance long way off
for now.
Far niente those loving lazy bears all
summer long.

Hérault sights, sounds, tastes and soft sand
in our toes,
a return to youth, hope and confidence
abound.

World beyond abundant with oysters galore,
magic pearl miracles,
provenance of that hazy Hérault all summer
long.

Romantic backdrops gestures freely given,
heart soaked in unusual abundance,
summers mirage no steadfast promises,
but feelings true.
Ease into flow of love, choosing happy.
A self-romance borne of felicità,
shaped by bear with his frolics and surprise
intents.

Bears at play basking and feasting,
a feeling founded in joy and love,
aware summer's predestined magnificence
glistens beyond.
A shining gem of a summer in lives borne of
times shaded and mediocre,
happiness for bears united in love and
comfort.
Never far from honey pot of heavenly truth,
that happiness truly is Hérault.

Rejuvenate French Rose Poetry Series

This third book in the **Rejuvenate French Rose Poetry Series – Happiness is Hérault,** as the title suggests a resting spot that brings great happiness. Fun times on holiday bringing a joy and a summer breeze that refreshes as well as lightens the soul's journey. The first book in the series **Perpignan Passion** has been inspired by trips to Perpignan and the Pyrénées-Orientales region. It's almost a mini travel guide for great places to visit in the area whilst sharing a few inspired moments where one is drawn to the spirit and light whilst indulging a romantic sensibility. Seeds are sown in the first poem for a dynastic romance novel that is currently bubbling away. The second book in the series is **St Tropez Senses**. As any visitor knows this place comes alive through all the senses of the body. A recollection of a holiday as a teenager is recalled whilst wandering as a solo visitor in later life. The intensity, inspiration and joy brought about from the sensory experiences here, set within a suite of sweet poems.

Rejuvenation Buddy Series

The Rejuvenation Buddy Series of mini guides for the modern woman have been developed to accompany you on your journey to your rejuvenated self. The concise narrative introduces topics in a light hearted way providing activities, tips and prompts in addition to introducing deeper concepts that may lead you to want to explore further the different aspects of the spiritual rejuvenation process.

The series is split into three parts - Build from Within, Celebrate Your Physical Body and Enjoy Your World. Each of the four buddy books within each part of the series are a kind of guide that distils a vast topic into a digestible mini read. Each book follows a standard format that includes:

The What – describing what the topic is all about,
The How to – explaining how to explore and develop your understanding and use of the topic,
The Joy in the Challenges – introducing the challenges and opportunities you are likely to encounter along the way and,
Feeling the Bliss – the icing on the cake, describing what success looks like.

The first to come in this series of mini reads in Part 1 – 'Build from Within' includes topics such as mindfulness from an authentic perspective, manifesting to bring magnificence into your life, thankfulness and managing your mind like a pilot navigating the sky.

Rejuvenate Rose Chic

The process of rejuvenation is intriguing and fundamental to those spiritual seekers looking to move towards the light as the spirit calls them. When sought via Rejuvenate Rose Chic it promises to be a joyful, fruitful and inspiring journey.

9 781913 560041